WORLD HISTORY

The Diagram Group

BROCKHAMPTON
DIAGRAM
GUIDES

World History

© Diagram Visual Information Ltd. 1997
  195 Kentish Town Road
  London
  NW5 2JU

First published in Great Britain in 1997 by
Brockhampton Press Ltd
20 Bloomsbury Street
London
WC1 2QA
a member of the Hodder Headline Group PLC

ISBN 1-86019-816-3

Also in this series:
Boxing Skills
Calligraphy
Card Games
Chinese Astrology
Drawing People
How the Body Works
Identifying Architecture
Kings and Queens of Britain
Magic Tricks
Origami
Party Games
Pub Games
SAS Survival Skills
Soccer Skills
Understanding Heraldry

Introduction

World History contains a wealth of fascinating information, starting with the history of the Earth itself and the first life forms.

Key events in history, landmarks in art and architecture, discoveries in science and inventions, and political and religious ideas are put into their chronological context. A snapshot overview of what was happening when and to whom, with many clear, informative illustrations.

Contents

History before man

4600 million years ago
The Earth starts to form from particles of dust, swirling gases, and tiny forming planets.

200 million years ago
The Earth has one large mass of land called Pangaea (**1**).

135 million years ago
The pieces of Pangaea start to break up. India becomes a separate landmass (**2**)

65 million years ago
The broken landmasses began to form the shapes of continents we recognize today (**3**).

Today
The Earth's continents are Asia, North America, South America, Australia, Europe, and Antarctica (**4**).

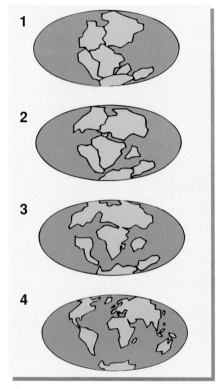

The geological timescale

The known history of the world is divided into four periods of time called eras: Precambrian, Paleozoic, Mesozoic, and Cenozoic. Eras are divided into periods, which in turn are divided into epochs. These divisions are based on various stages in the development of life shown in fossils. The length of eras, periods and epochs are not equal. A chart showing the Earth's history by using the different time divisions is called a geological timescale. The Earth's earliest history is shown at the bottom and the most recent at the top. This matches how rocks are formed, with the oldest at the bottom and the youngest at the top.

Era millions of years ago	Period	Epoch
Cenozoic 65-present	Quaternary 2-present	Holocene 0.01-present
		Pleistocene 2-0.01
	Tertiary 65-2	Pliocene 5-2
		Miocene 24.6-5
		Oligocene 38-24.6
		Eocene 55-38
		Paleocene 65-55
Mesozoic 248-65	Cretaceous 144-65	
	Jurassic 213-144	
	Triassic 248-213	
Palaeozoic 540-248	Permian 286-248	
	*Carboniferous 360-286	
	Devonian 408-360	
	Silurian 440-408	
	Ordovician 505-440	
	Cambrian 540-505	
Precambrian before 540		

* Mississippian and Pennsylvanian periods in N. America

The first life forms

Fossils found in rocks of different ages show how living things evolved, or changed, through time. The first life forms were microscopically tiny organisms. Later came soft-bodied sea creatures. Some of these gave rise to animals with shells or inner skeletons. Fishes gave rise to amphibians. Amphibians led on to reptiles, a group of animals which separated into birds and mammals.

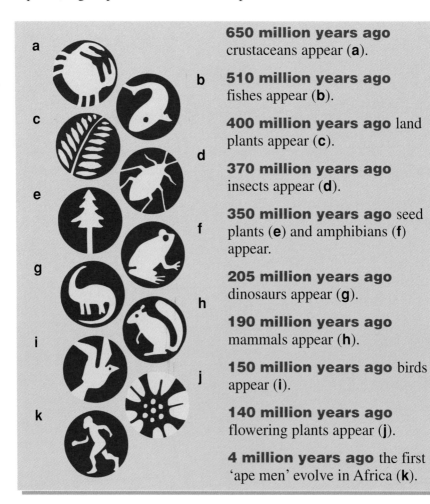

650 million years ago crustaceans appear (**a**).

510 million years ago fishes appear (**b**).

400 million years ago land plants appear (**c**).

370 million years ago insects appear (**d**).

350 million years ago seed plants (**e**) and amphibians (**f**) appear.

205 million years ago dinosaurs appear (**g**).

190 million years ago mammals appear (**h**).

150 million years ago birds appear (**i**).

140 million years ago flowering plants appear (**j**).

4 million years ago the first 'ape men' evolve in Africa (**k**).

The first humans

4 million years ago *Australopithecus afarensis* ('southern ape of Afar'), the first known 'ape man' evolved in Africa. They were hairy creatures, some slightly built and no bigger than a chimpanzee, others muscular and nearer modern-man size.

3 million years ago *Australopithecus africanus* ('southern ape of Africa') lived. They were small, slight, ape-like creatures as tall as a small African bushman and weighing no more than a 12-year-old European girl.

2.5 million years ago *Australopithecus robustus* a larger and stronger creature than *Australopithecus africanus* lived. *Australopithecus boisei*, a more massive version of *Australopithecus robustus*, also lived.

2 million years ago *Homo habilis* ('handy man') lived, with a larger brain than *Australopithecus* and a smaller, less projecting face.

1.6 million years ago *Homo erectus* ('upright man') lived, with a bigger brain than *Homo habilis*, a flatter face than ours, projecting jaws and strong muscles at the back of the neck.

200,000 years ago *Homo sapiens neanderthalensis* lived; short and stocky, with large joints and hands and a powerful, chinless jaw.

40,000 years ago *Homo sapiens sapiens* lived; early modern man, with smaller jaws and more crowded teeth than its ancestors and a well-developed chin.

6000 BC–1 AD

c. 2000–1500 BC Egyptian civilization at the height of its power and achievements.

c. 1200 BC Israelites, led by Moses, leave Egypt and settle in Canaan (Israel).

776 BC Olympic Games founded in ancient Greece.

753 BC City of Rome founded in Italy.

100 BC Birth of Julius Caesar who becomes a great Roman general.

69 BC Birth of Cleopatra who becomes Queen of Egypt and marries Mark Antony.

4 BC Probable date of Jesus's birth.

c. 2500 BC Egyptians build Great Sphinx, a huge monument with the head of a Pharaoh and a lion's body.

c. 2100 BC Stonehenge built in England.

447 BC Athenians begin building the Parthenon, a temple to goddess Athena.

215 BC Chinese begin building Great Wall.

c. **6000 BC** Bricks used in Jericho.

c. **4000 BC** Saw used in Egypt.

c. **3500 BC** Sumerian civilization invents cuneiform (wedge-shaped) writing.

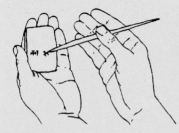

c. **3480 BC** Sumerians invent the wheel and use oar-propelled ships.

c. **2500 BC** Soap used by Sumerians.

c. **1300 BC** Parchment used by Egyptians.

c. **400 BC** Greek scientist Hippocrates develops knowledge of medicine.

c. **200 BC** Romans invent concrete.

c. **1500 BC** Hindu religion develops in India.

c. **1200 BC** Death of Moses who, by tradition, wrote down the word of God in the Jewish Bible.

c. **521 BC** Buddha, founder of Buddhism, preaches his first sermon in India.

Greek philosophers

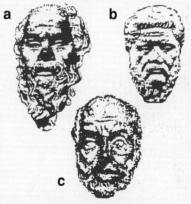

a Socrates (469–399 BC), once declared to be the wisest man alive.

b Plato (c. 427–c. 347 BC), one of western civilization's most important philosophers.

c Aristotle (384–322 BC), influential scientist and philosopher, develops logical forms of argument.

© DIAGRAM

1AD–1000

c. 4 BC–30 AD Life of Jesus Christ.

30 Romans crucify Jesus.
43 Roman invasion of Britain.
117 Roman Empire at maximum extent.
c. 250 Golden age of Mayan culture begins. Mayans build their homes and pyramidal temples from limestone. They carve important dates on stone using picture writing.

537 Death of Arthur, a semi-legendary king of the Britons.
742–814 Charlemagne, King of the Franks promotes education and the arts.
840 The start of important Viking expeditions.

10 AD Great Wall of China completed. This runs for nearly 1,500 mi (over 2,400 km) and is at least 20 ft (7 m high). Six horsemen abreast can ride along it.
70 The Colosseum is built in Rome. This huge arena, large enough to seat 50,000 viewers, is the scene of battles between gladiators.

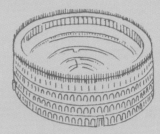

c. 122–7 Hadrian's Wall built in Britain.

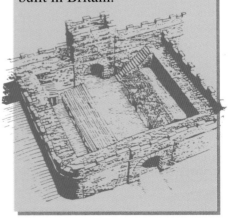

c. 100 AD Romans use central heating.
105 Paper invented in China.

c. 190 Use of abacus in China, man's first calculator.

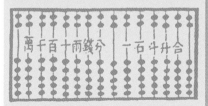

850 Navigational device called the astrolabe perfected by Arab astronomers.
900 Gunpowder invented by the Chinese to make fireworks.
c. 900 Windmill first used in Persia.
983 Canal lock invented by Chaiao Wei-Yo.

50–150 AD The Christian New Testament composed.
380 Christianity is the official religion of the Roman Empire.
c. 380 Hinduism in South East Asia.
c. 550 Buddhism in Japan.

622 Mohammed founds the Muslim faith.
700 First Buddhist monastery built in Tibet.

The beginnings of scholasticism
The works of ancient Greek and Roman philosophers come to the attention of Western Europe whose scholars spend much time investigating the ideas of Aristotle. The attempt by medieval scholars to reconcile what the church said with what Aristotle said is often called *scholasticism*.

1000–1200

1066 Norman invasion of England.

1066 Battle of Hastings.
1086 The Domesday Book compiled in England.
1095 Start of the Crusades, military expeditions formed of Christian armies recapture the Holy Lands from the Muslim Turks.

c. 1162 Birth of Genghis Khan, a skilful administrator and ruler who unites Mongol tribes and conquers empires.

1000 Between 1000 and 1100 towns in Europe begin to build massive stone churches.
1052 Work begins on Westminster Abbey in London.
1077 The Bayeux Tapestry completed in France.
1081 Work begins on the Tower of London.

c. 1150 Angkor Wat built in Cambodia, a temple to the Hindu god Vishnu that is more than half a mile long.
1163 Work starts on the huge Gothic cathedral of Notre Dame in Paris.

The flying buttress is an invention that helps with the building of huge stone churches and cathedrals. Heavy stone roofs push outward and downward, and to support the outward pressure Gothic builders make beautifully carved supports called *flying buttresses* which slant up against the outside walls of cathedrals and churches.

1025 Paper money used in China.
1050 Compass used by Chinese and Arabs.
1080 Earliest stained glass used in Germany.

1054 Formal separation between Orthodox (eastern) and Roman Catholic (western) Churches.

The Church
By the 1100s the church is ruled very much like a kingdom, with a ruler (the Pope) from the capital (Rome). Outside Rome, power of the church is in the hands of Bishops.

Chivalry
During the 1100s a code of conduct for knights is developed, known as chivalry. Chivalry requires a knight to be courteous to women, to be brave and to fight fairly. He also has to be loyal to his friends and to treat conquered foes gallantly.

1200–1400

1215 Magna Carta signed in England, a document protecting the rights of noblemen but also of England's ordinary people.

1325 The Aztecs build their capital city, Tenochtitlán in Mexico.

1338 Hundred Years' War begins between France and England.

1346–49 A plague known as The Black Death sweeps through Europe.

c. 1390 Inca Empire develops in modern-day South America.

1300 Passion plays are staged in Europe depicting the last days of Christ's life on Earth.

1321 Italian poet Dante Alighieri writes a long poem about Heaven and Hell, called *The Divine Comedy*.

c. 1350 The Leaning Tower of Pisa is finished.

1387 English poet Geoffrey Chaucer starts *The Canterbury Tales*, a collection of tales told by pilgrims journeying to Canterbury in England.

1249 Spectacles appear in China and Europe.

1264 Bakers' marks – icons slashed on bread – are used by bakers to identify their wares. They are the forerunners of trademarks.

c. 1265 Japanese swordsmiths create tachi (slashing swords) that are sharp enough to behead an enemy with one stroke.

1276 Papermaking begins in Italy.

1288 Gun invented in China.

1291 Glassmakers learn to produce clear glass. Glass up until now had always been coloured.

1300 Mechanical clocks are invented in Europe.

1320 Paper reaches Europe for the first time and replaces vellum, a parchment made from the skin of animals.

1360 Development of stringed keyboard instruments – the clavichord and harpsichord.

The Inquisition
In the 1200s there is widespread interest in religion. Some people hold beliefs that are different from those of the Christian church, and these people are known as heretics. Heretics are slaughtered by the church when discovered. The job of finding and judging heretics falls to a group called the Inquisition.

1225 The Christian church sends members of the Inquisition throughout Europe to search out heretics. People suspected of heresy can be questioned for many weeks and are often tortured.

1300 The Renaissance begins in Italy. During this time men and women in Italy hope to renew interest in the classical culture of Greek and Rome.

© DIAGRAM

1400–1500

1415 Henry V of England invades France and wins the Battle of Agincourt.

1431 Joan of Arc, a peasant girl who leads the resistance against the English, is tried for heresy and sorcery and burned at the stake.

1492 Christopher Columbus, an Italian mariner, crosses the Atlantic and discovers the New World. He is the first European since the Vikings to reach the Americas.

1492 Jews and Muslims driven out of Spain.

1400s A flat board with a hole for the thumb, used for arranging paints (a palette), first appears in Europe.

1440s In the Aztec city of Tenochtitlán, Mexico, a new style of picture sculpture emerges.

1490 Dance performances take place in France, Bulgaria and Italy at festive occasions and are the origins of ballet.

1498 Albrecht Dürer, a German painter and engraver publishes a series of especially fine woodcuts. Dürer becomes famous for his engravings, drawings and paintings.

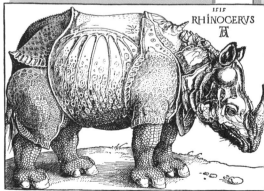

1450 The arquebus, a Dutch firearm, is the first effective firearm small enough to be fired by a single person.

c. 1450 Moveable type process invented in Germany replaces printing using wooden blocks and fixed lettering.

1469 Sikhism founded. Nanak is an Indian who lives between 1469 and 1539. He is a thinker who later becomes a guru of a new religion called Sikhism. Nanak's teachings combine ideas from both Islam and Hindu. His followers are known as Sikhs, meaning 'disciples'.

The Renaissance
Between 1400 and 1500 Renaissance ideas spread from Italy to the rest of Europe. The movement emphasized the importance of the individual, of education, of free thought, and acceptance of classical Greek and Latin art and literature as models.

c. 1450 The practice of bloodletting, leeching, purging and cupping are common medical practices in Europe.
1456 First Bible printed.
c. 1480 Alchemy, the process of trying to turn metal into gold, becomes the science of chemistry.

1400–1500 New universities develop throughout Europe.

1500–1600

Slave trade
During the 1500s, about 2,000 slaves are transported from Africa each year. To prevent them from jumping overboard they are chained in the overcrowded holds of ships and many die before reaching their destination.

1507 The name America appears on a map for the first time.
1522 The Spanish discover the Inca Empire.
1526 The Mughal Empire founded in India.
1556 A devastating earthquake kills hundreds of thousands of people in China.
1588 A fleet of 130 Spanish ships called the Armada is defeated in the English Channel by Francis Drake.

1503 The *Mona Lisa* is painted by Leonardo da Vinci.
1564–1616 William Shakespeare, a poet and playwright living in London, writes 37 plays including *Romeo and Juliet*, *Hamlet* and *The Merchant of Venice*.

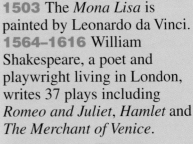

1576 The first permanent theatre is built in London.
1599 The Globe theatre opens in London, the largest Elizabethan playhouse.

The High Renaissance
Between 1500 and 1520 there is a period of great achievement in painting and sculpture known as the High Renaissance, dominated by artists such as Leonardo da Vinci, Michelangelo, and Raphael.

c. 1500 Ambroise Paré devises artificial limbs for injured soldiers.

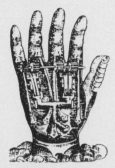

1565 Pencil invented.
1578 William Harvey, an English physician, establishes that the heart is a muscle and that blood circulates.

1590 Microscope invented.
1596 Invention of the water closet to replace the chamber pot and privy.

The Reformation
Around 1500, some people argue that the Roman Catholic church has lost sight of the spiritual mission proclaimed by Jesus and a generation of reformers urge people to form a new church. This religious revolution is called the Reformation. People who protest against the existing church are called Protestants, one of the most well known of whom is Martin Luther.

Witch hunting
During the 1500s there was an outburst of witch hunting. Many thousands of innocent women (and men) were accused and burned alive.

1600–1700

1605 The Gunpowder Plot, an unsuccessful conspiracy to blow up the English King James I and his Parliament.
1620 Nonconformists (dissenters from the Church of England) known as the Pilgrim Fathers, sail in the *Mayflower* from Plymouth, England, to settle in America.

1642–6 English Civil War between Royalist forces of Charles I and Parliamentarians under Oliver Cromwell.
1650 Wars between European settlers and North American Indians.
1680 The last dodo dies on the island of Mauritius in the Indian ocean having been exterminated by Dutch settlers.

1600s The Kabuki theatre develops in Japan. Performers wear beautiful costumes and, accompanied by music and clappers, perform contemporary and historical plays and dances.
1600s Huge figures carved of rock are lined up on Easter Island in the Pacific.

1605 *Don Quixote de la Mancha* by the Spanish novelist and playwright Miguel de Cervantes is published.

1648 The Taj Mahal, a massive mausoleum, is built in India.

1610 Italian scientist Galileo makes important discoveries regarding the stars and planets using a telescope.

1612 American colonists learn to grow tobacco and export it to England.
1623 Adding machine invented.
1635 Mail is delivered between London and Edinburgh by wheeled coaches.
1644 Barometer invented.
1650 Air pump invented.
1654 Slide rule invented.
1657 Pendulum clock invented.
1682 Edmund Halley observes a comet that is later named after him.
1688 Large sheets of glass are used in France for making windows and mirrors.
1689 Steam pump invented.

1611 A new English translation of the Bible, authorized by King James I, is published and is known as the King James Bible.

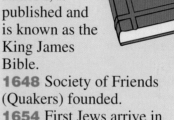

1648 Society of Friends (Quakers) founded.
1654 First Jews arrive in America.

Philosophers of science

During the 1600s the ideas of astronomers, scientists and philosophers like Copernicus, Galileo, Brahe, Descartes and Kepler change the way people view the world. A number of non-scientists, such as Sir Frances Bacon, argue in favour of scientists making new discoveries that are free from the ignorance and prejudice of the past. Important philosophers are Hobbes and Locke who write about matters relating to politics and government.

1700–1800

1715 Total solar eclipse, visible in Britain and parts of Europe.
1755 A huge earthquake strikes Lisbon in Portugal, sparking interest in geological phenomena.
1758 Return of the 1682 comet as predicted by Edmund Halley.
1760 In London, the Kew Botanical Gardens open.
1774 Marie Antoinette becomes Queen of France.
1775–83 American War of Independence.

1781 An outbreak of smallpox among Spanish settlers in Texas sweeps North America and more than 130,000 native Americans die.
1789 French Revolution begins.

1700s To help indicate the age and appearance of characters, actors in Europe wear powder makeup, usually mixed with a sort of liquid grease.
1719 English novelist Daniel Defoe writes *Robinson Crusoe*, based on the true story of a shipwrecked sailor called Alexander Selkirk.

1726 *Gulliver's Travels* by Anglo-Irish satirist Jonathan Swift is published.
1770–1827 German composer Ludwig van Beethoven is completely deaf in the last decade of his life but still composes magnificent works.
1787 Austrian Wolfgang Amadeus Mozart composes the opera *Don Giovanni*.

1708–9 In Europe, the method for producing porcelain is discovered at Meissen, Germany.
1712 Piston steam engine invented.
1714 Mercury thermometer invented.
1718 Machine gun invented.
1761 The first veterinary school is founded in France.
1764 Spinning jenny invented.

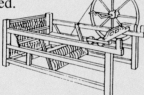

1769 Steam engine invented.
1774 The element oxygen is discovered.
1775 The flush toilet is patented.
1781 The first all-iron bridge opens in England. Weighing 378 tons it spans over 30 m (100 ft).
1784 Gas lighting invented.
1792 Opening of The Mint of the United States to produce coins based on the decimal system.

Enlightenment Era (Age of Reason)
During the 1700s a group of philosophers argue that people could apply reason to all areas of their life. Amongst them is French writer Voltaire, who is frequently imprisoned and exiled. He attacks social pretensions, political and social injustices, and religious intolerance.

1774 The Quakers, a religious sect from England, settle in the American colonies.
1776 Publication of *The Wealth of Nations* by Scottish economist Adam Smith.

© DIAGRAM

1800–1820

1801 The Union Jack becomes the official flag of the United Kingdom of Great Britain and Ireland.

1805 Battle of Trafalgar. British admiral Nelson defeats the Franco-Spanish fleet.
1808 America prohibits the importation of slaves from Africa.
1815 Battle of Waterloo. Napoleon (Emperor of France) defeated by British and Prussian forces under the Duke of Wellington.

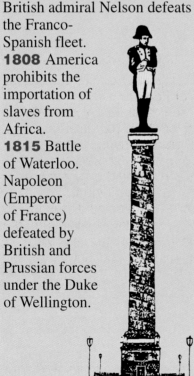

1809–49 Edgar Allan Poe, American poet and writer, completes many macabre short stories including *The Fall of the House of Usher* and the detective story *Murders in the Rue Morgue*.

1813 Jane Austen, English novelist, publishes *Pride and Prejudice*.

1814 Franz Schubert, an Austrian composer, begins a prolific period of music composition.
1818 Publication of British writer Mary Shelley's *Frankenstein*.
1820 The statue Venus de Milo is discovered on the Greek island of Melos.

1802 First icebox invented, forerunner of the refrigerator.
1803 Coal gas for factory lighting invented.
1804 Automatic loom invented in France.
1804 Steam railway locomotive invented in England.

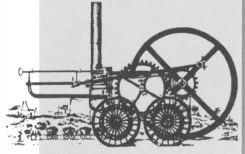

1807 First commercial steamboat built in US.

1807 Street lighting by gas in London.
1814 First commercially sold tinned food is produced in England.
1816 Stethoscope invented.

Nationalism
During the 1800s there is a growth in nationalism. Nationalists believe that a person should be loyal to their nation-state. Millions of Europeans adopt this view and strive to unite people with a similar history, language and traditions to become one nation with a single government.

Political divisions
The French Revolution leads to the development of liberalism, conservatism and radicalism. Liberals support the movement to give more power to parliament, conservatives believe in protecting the existing form of government, and radicals favour drastic change.

© DIAGRAM

1820–1850

1824 The first dinosaur to be described is *Megalosaurus*, identified from fossils in England.

1825 A second dinosaur is discovered and is called *Iguanodon*.

1837 Accession of Queen Victoria in Britain. Britain leads the Industrial Revolution.

1845 Irish potato famine begins.
1847 In America, first adhesive postage stamps used.

1835 Completion of the Arc de Triomphe in Paris.

1837 English novelist Charles Dickens publishes *The Adventures of Oliver Twist*.

1835–72 Hans Christian Andersen, a Danish writer, publishes what are to become popular fairy tales.

1844 French novelist and playwright Alexandre Dumas père (father) publishes *The Three Musketeers*.

1825 First steam train passenger service in England.

1831 Telegraph invented in England.
1834 Braille invented.
1839 Bicycle invented.

1839 Development of the first commercially viable photographic process, the daguerreotype.
1845 An American dentist produces the first single porcelain tooth.
1847 The explosive nitroglycerine is first produced.
1849 America's first female physician graduates from Geneva College of Medicine in New York.

1822 The Roman Catholic Church finally lifts its ban on the works of astronomers Copernicus, Galileo, and Kepler.
1847 Publication of *The Communist Manifesto* by Karl Marx, a German philosopher and economist who laid the foundations for communism. He is also the auther of *Das Kapital*.

Belief in phrenology
Despite evidence to the contrary, phrenology – the belief that you can tell a person's personality from the bumps on their head – persists at this time.

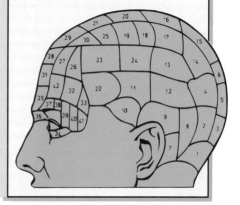

© DIAGRAM

1850–1870

1853–6 Crimean War between Russia and Britain, France and the Ottoman (Turkish) Empire.

Florence Nightingale
Florence Nightingale, a British philanthropist, arrives in Constantinople with 38 other volunteers caring for the sick and injured soldiers of the Crimean War, she later becomes known as the founder of modern nursing.

1860 The first nurse-training school established in London by Florence Nightingale.
1861–5 American Civil War.

1851 The Great Exhibition in London, a world fair in a specially constructed Crystal Palace in Hyde Park.
1851 American novelist Herman Melville publishes *Moby Dick*.
1862 Victor Hugo, French poet and novelist, produces *Les Misérables*.

1864 Completion of the Houses of Parliament in London.
1865 Publication of *Alice's Adventures in Wonderland* by Lewis Carroll, an English maths don.

1869 Leo Tolstoy, Russian novelist, publishes *War and Peace*.

1851 Sewing machine invented.
1854 Life size models of dinosaurs on public display at Crystal Palace, in London.
1858 One of the most famous books of anatomy published, *Anatomy*, by Henry Gray.
1861 Pneumatic drill invented.
1862 Refrigerator invented.
1866 Whilst experimenting with pea plants, Austrian monk Gregor J. Mendel discovers that an organism's traits are determined from hereditary units called genes. His work forms the basics of the science of genetics.
1867 Dynamite invented.
1868 Typewriter invented.

Evolution
In 1859, English naturalist Charles Darwin publishes *On the Origin of Species* in which he sets out his highly controversial theory of evolution. Darwin argues that as individuals adapt to their environment, new species emerge and replace less well adapted individuals.

1865 The Salvation Army is established by William Booth.

© DIAGRAM

1870–1900

1870–71 Germany defeats France in the Franco-Prussian War.
1871 German Empire founded with Bismarck as Chancellor.
1872 In America 51 women are arrested for trying to vote in the presidential election.
1876 Díaz becomes dictator in Mexico.
c. 1880 The world's first social security system is established in Germany.
1882 British take control of Egypt.
1896 The Olympic Games are revived.

1899 First Hague Peace Conference fails to stop escalating arms production in Europe.

1876 The American writer Mark Twain publishes *The Adventures of Tom Sawyer.*
1883 Scottish novelist Robert Louis Stevenson publishes *Treasure Island.*
1886 Statue of Liberty constructed in New York.
1887 British novelist Arthur Conan Doyle publishes *The Hound of the Baskervilles.*
1889 Completion of the Eiffel Tower in Paris.

1890 Dutch Vincent van Gogh paints *Self Portrait.*
1895 H.G. Wells, English novelist, publishes *The Time Machine.*
1897 Publication of *Dracula,* by Irish novelist Bram Stoker.

1870 Plastics (celluloid) invented.
1876 Telephone invented by Alexander Graham Bell.
1877 The first phonograph is tested. Invented by Thomas Edison it plays back 'Mary had a Little Lamb.'
1879 Electric light bulb invented.
1883 Skyscraper invented.
1884 Fountain pen invented.
1884 The first building with a steel frame is constructed, in Chicago, America.
1885 Automobiles first produced.

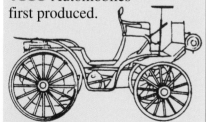

1887 Contact lens invented.
1895 X-rays first used.

Imperialism
Imperialism is the policy of conquering and ruling other lands. During the late 1880s, colonies are seen as being essential for economic well-being and countries such as France, Britain, Spain, Portugal, Austria-Hungary and Russia expand their empires. Countries without colonies (such as Belgium, Italy and Germany) set out to acquire them.

Women's movement
In the 1870s most countries in Western Europe had given most men the right to vote. Reformers around this time begin to demand equal voting rights for women. In 1888 the International Council for Women is founded by activists in Great Britain, which becomes the centre for the women's movement.

VOTES FOR WOMEN

1900–1920

1905 'Bloody Sunday' in Russia. 1,000 people are murdered when they petition the czar for better working conditions.

1910 Revolution in Mexico.

1912–13 The Ottoman (Turkish) Empire loses its European territory in the Balkan Wars.

1914 World War I starts when Germany declares war on Russia and France.

1917 Lenin (Vladimir Ilyich) leads the Russian Revolution.

1918 IRA (Irish Republican Army) formed to fight British occupation of Ireland.

1918–20 Civil War in Russia. About 15 million Russians die, many from starvation.

Charlie Chaplin
Charles Chaplin is a British-born comedian and star of early silent movies. In his most famous films he plays a scruffy little-man with a bowler hat, a cane and a silly walk.

1910 Spanish Pablo Picasso paints *Girl with Mandolin*.

1913 Igor Stravinsky, Russian composer, produces his revolutionary ballet score *The Rite of Spring*.

1913 French author, Marcel Proust, produces the first part of *Remembrance of Things Past*, a novel that is to profoundly influence the development of modern literature.

1900 Airship invented by Ferdinand von Zeppelin.
1901 Vacuum cleaner invented.
1903 Airplane invented by Orville and Wilbur Wright.

1906 Use of the first gramophone with an integral horn, the Victor Victoria.
1907 Washing machine invented.
1910 First radio broadcast.
1911 Development of IQ tests.
1912 Stainless steel invented.
1913 Charles Fabry, a French physicist, proves the existence of the ozone layer.
1915 First use of poisonous gas as a military weapon.
1916 Tank invented.
1917 Sonar developed, a method for detecting underwater objects.
1918 The pop-up toaster patented in America.
1919 The first nonstop transatlantic flight.

c. 1920 Rastafarianism established in Jamaica. The movement is named after Ras Tafari who became Emperor of Ethiopia. Rastafarianism is more a way of life than a religion. It is guided by the culture and traditions of Ethiopia with a unity and pride in African heritage.

Soviet Communism
Under Lenin Communists believe in a worldwide revolution to overthrow capitalist societies, and produce a classless, equal society. Between 1917 and 1920 all means of economic production, including agriculture, are taken over by the state. Small farms are merged to create vast, collective, state-run farms and a policy of rapid industrialisation is adopted to match the output of Western powers.

1920–1930

1920 Start of prohibition. Legislation against the sale of alcohol in America, leads to illicit sales and gangsterism.

1921 United Kingdom of Great Britain and Northern Ireland formed.

1922 Union of Soviet Socialist Republics (USSR) formed.

1922 The English archaeologist Howard Carter discovers the ancient Egyptian tomb of King Tutankhamen.

1929 The Wall Street Crash leads to worldwide economic depression.

Laurel and Hardy
The team of Stan Laurel and Oliver Hardy are popular early film comedians.

The Marx Brothers
An American comedy team who make several films during the early 1900s. They are brothers known as Chico, Harpo, Groucho, and Zeppo. A fifth member, Gummo, was originally part of their live act.

1922 James Joyce, Irish novelist, publishes *Ulysses*.

1927 *The Jazz Singer*, with Al Jolson, is the first 'talkie' film.

1925 Television invented by John Logie Baird.

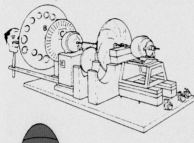

1926 Rocket invented.
1928 Antibiotics developed by Alexander Fleming.

1928 First transatlantic flight is made by balloon airship called the *Graf Zeppelin*.

1929 Frozen foods invented.
1930s The German autobahn system is developed, the first modern national expressway system.

Stalinism
In 1929 Joseph Stalin becomes dictator of the Soviet Union. He supports the idea of a Communist state with a classless society, collectivized agriculture, and common ownership of property. He sets about eliminating possible challengers to his total control of government. Many Communist Party members suspected of treason are executed and many are deported to labour camps.

1930–1940

1933 Austrian born Adolf Hitler is appointed Chancellor of Germany. He leads the Nazi Party and is a ruthless dictator who institutes ferocious anti-Semitic policies and is given the title Führer (leader).

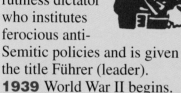

1939 World War II begins.

1940 Jews in German-occupied countries are rounded up and sent to forced-labour camps.

1932 Completion of the Empire State Building in New York.

1937 JRR Tolkein, a British novelist publishes *The Hobbit*, a fantasy novel.

1937 Spanish Pablo Picasso paints *Guernica*, considered to be one of his masterpieces.

1938 Superman appears in Action Comics No. 1.

1938 An American called Orson Welles performs *War of the Worlds*, a radio play that is so realistic many listeners believe their country is being invaded by aliens.

1939 John Wayne establishes himself as a Hollywood star of popular westerns.

c. **1930** Use of snorkels.
1931 Amphibious tank invented.
1931 Vitamin A first identified.
c. **1932** Iron lung, an artificial respirator, invented.
1933 Electron microscope invented.
1933 Detergents developed.
1933 Influenza virus isolated.
1933 Radioactive isotopes produced.
1934 Cat's-eyes traffic aid invented.

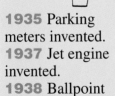

1935 Parking meters invented.
1937 Jet engine invented.
1938 Ballpoint pen invented.
1938 Nuclear fission (atom splitting) discovered.
1938 Nylon invented.
1939 First helicopters built.

Gandhi

Mohandras Gandhi called Mahatma 'Great Soul' is an Indian patriot, social reformer, and moral teacher. He lives in South Africa until 1914 then returns to India and leads the independence movement. He attempts to rid India of the caste system (an extreme system of classes in Indian society) and works to unite Hindus and Muslims.

Fascism

Fear of communist revolution and frustrated national ambitions following World War I encourages the growth of Fascism, especially under Mussolini in Italy and Hitler and the Nazi party. Hitler's policies reject ideas of individual liberty and equality and support national superiority, militarism and anti-Semitism.

1940–1950

1941 Japan bombs Pearl Harbor.

1941–45 Six million Jews murdered by German Nazis in the Holocaust.

1942 Under Hitler, Germany embarks on the 'Final Solution' – the systematic removal of Jews, gypsies, homosexuals, Communists and dissenters.

1945 Germany surrenders. World War II ends after atomic bombs dropped on Hiroshima and Nagasaki in Japan.

1946–49 Cold War begins as Western European nations ally with the United States against Communist Eastern Europe and the Soviet Union. Fear of nuclear war prevents military confrontation.

1947 *The Dead Sea Scrolls* are discovered in Israel, religious texts about ancient Judaism and Christianity.

1942 The film *Casablanca* is released with Humphrey Bogart and Ingrid Bergman.

1943 The Pentagon is finished in America. At 6.5 million square feet, it is the largest building in the world.

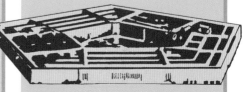

1946 Marcel Marceau, a French actor and mime artist portrays a character called Bip which is to make him famous throughout the world.

1949 English novelist George Orwell publishes his pessimistic view of the future, *Nineteen Eighty Four*.

1940 First servicable helicopter.

1940 Nylon stockings sold for the first time in America.

1944 First digital computer completed.

1945 Atomic bomb invented.

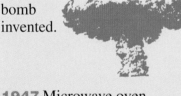

1947 Microwave oven invented.

1948 Long-play record invented.

1948 Electronic computer invented.

1948 Transistor radio invented, replacing valve radios.

The Ecumenical Movement
This is a movement to promote closer contact and understanding between Christian Churches. In 1948 the World Council of Churches is formed which aims to reduce differences in doctrine and encourage Christian unity.

Anti-Semitism
Hostility towards Jews reaches its peak under Hitler. The Nazis believe that German 'Aryans' are a superior race and that Jews are inferior.

1950–1960

1950–53 US intervene in an indecisive conflict between Communist and non-Communist forces in Korea.

1952 Elizabeth II becomes Queen of Great Britain.

1957 European Economic Community (EEC) founded to promote economic development in Europe.

1959 Communist Castro takes power in Cuba.

1951 Festival of Britain – a celebration of the end of rationing and other wartime and postwar austerity measures.

Marilyn Monroe American actress becomes a popular sex symbol after starring in films such as *Gentlemen Prefer Blondes* (1953), and *Some Like it Hot* (1959).

1954 Elvis Presley, an American singer records his first commercially successful record and later becomes a worldwide star.

1955 James Dean, an American actor dies in a car crash after achieving stardom in films like *Rebel Without a Cause* and *East of Eden*.

c. 1960 Andy Warhol, American pop artist and film producer, achieves fame with paintings of soup cans and of Marilyn Monroe.

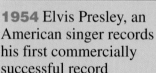
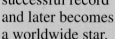

1952 World's first jet passenger airliner, the De Havilland Comet, enters service.

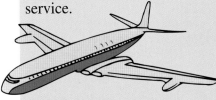

1953 Structure of the DNA molecule described.
1955 Nonstick pan invented.
1955 Contraceptive pill developed.
1956 Video recorder invented.
1956 World's first nuclear power station opens in England.
1957 Heart pacemaker invented.
1957 Soviet Sputnik; world's first satellite.

1959 Hovercraft invented.

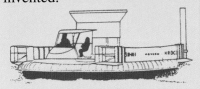

Consumerism
The idea that consumers should influence the quality and prices of goods and services develops in the 1950s. In the UK, The Consumer's Association is established in 1957 to carry out tests on consumer goods on the consumers' behalf.

Existentialism
This philosophical movement is concerned with the individual's experience and existence in the world. It is developed by French intellectuals especially Sartre, after World War II.

1960–PRESENT DAY

1961 Berlin Wall built between Communist East Berlin and non-Communist West Berlin to stem the flood of over 2 million refugees heading west.

1963 President Kennedy assassinated in American city, Dallas.

1964 Nelson Mandela and other African National Congress and Pan-African Congress leaders are given life jail sentences. Mandela is a South African Black Nationalist leader and lawyer who advocates multiracial democracy and non-violent protest.
1965–75 Vietnam War between Communist north and non-Communist south Vietnam.

1969 First man on the moon.
1982 Falklands War between the UK and Argentina.
1986 Chernobyl nuclear power station explodes.
1989 Berlin Wall demolished.
1990 Nelson Mandela freed.

1990 Gulf War begins after Iraq invades Kuwait.

1990 East and West Germany re-united.
1991 Disintegration of the USSR.
1991–6 Civil War fragments Yugoslavia.

1960 Alfred Hitchcock directs the fast-paced thriller film *Psycho*.

1961 Benjamin Britten's *War Requiem*, commemorating the dead of World War II, is regarded as one of the finest works of modern music.
1963 The Beatles, an English pop group are topping the British charts with every single they release and are to become the world's most famous pop group.

1967 David Hockney, pop artist, paints *A Bigger Splash*.

1969 In America, The Woodstock Music and Art Fair attracts more than 400,000 people for 3 days of 'peace, love and music'.
1976 Disco becomes a popular music form.
1982 The singer and performer Michael Jackson releases LP *Thriller*, which spends 37 weeks at the top of the US chart and sells over 40 million copies worldwide.

1991 The controversial singer Madonna causes a storm when she releases a tour film *Truth or Dare (In Bed With Madonna)* featuring sexually provocative scenes.

1960 Laser invented.
1960 Mini computer invented.
1960 The first weather satellite is launched.
1965 Word processor invented.
1966 Artificial blood invented.
1970 Floppy disc invented.
1973 Skylab is launched, the first orbiting space station.

1978 Compact disc invented.
1978 The first test-tube baby is born.
1981 Space shuttle invented.

1982 The term AIDS (Acquired Immune Deficiency Syndrome) is used to describe a fatal immune system disorder.
1993 Human embryos are cloned.

Creationists
In 1960s America a group of people known as creationists advocate that God created all life forms, and reject Darwin's theory of evolution.

The Green Movement
In the 1970s many people are concerned with the environment and with environmental damage. The Green Movement develops.

The Peace Movement
During the 1960s and 1970s the Peace Movement develops when many people are horrified by the build-up of atomic weapons and the threat of nuclear war.